The Dweller Of The Threshold And

How Fear May Be Defeated

William Walker Atkinson

Kessinger Publishing's Rare Reprints

Thousands of Scarce and Hard-to-Find Books on These and other Subjects!

- Americana
- Ancient Mysteries
- Animals
- Anthropology
- Architecture
- Arts
- Astrology
- Bibliographies
- Biographies & Memoirs
- Body, Mind & Spirit
- Business & Investing
- Children & Young Adult
- Collectibles
- Comparative Religions
- Crafts & Hobbies
- Earth Sciences
- Education
- Ephemera
- Fiction
- Folklore
- Geography
- Health & Diet
- History
- Hobbies & Leisure
- Humor
- Illustrated Books
- Language & Culture
- Law
- Life Sciences

- Literature
- Medicine & Pharmacy
- Metaphysical
- Music
- Mystery & Crime
- Mythology
- Natural History
- Outdoor & Nature
- Philosophy
- Poetry
- Political Science
- Science
- Psychiatry & Psychology
- Reference
- Religion & Spiritualism
- Rhetoric
- Sacred Books
- Science Fiction
- Science & Technology
- Self-Help
- Social Sciences
- Symbolism
- Theatre & Drama
- Theology
- Travel & Explorations
- War & Military
- Women
- Yoga
- *Plus Much More!*

**We kindly invite you to view our catalog list at:
http://www.kessinger.net**

THIS ARTICLE WAS EXTRACTED FROM THE BOOK:

Law of the New Thought: A Study of Fundamental Principles and Their Application

BY THIS AUTHOR:

William Walker Atkinson

ISBN 1564598462

CHAPTER V.

THE DWELLER OF THE THRESHOLD.

Bulwer Lytton's creation—The frightful monster confronting the neophyte in the secret chamber—The real meaning of the occult figure of speech—Fear the great obstacle to success and happiness, and spiritual attainment—Stands at the door to Freedom—Keeps the race in bondage—No advancement possible until it is overcome—And it can be overcome—Confront it boldly and it retreats—Assert the I Am—Fear is as much a magnet as Desire—Fear the parent of all the brood of negative thought—Illustrations—Fear has hypnotized the race—Fear never did Man any good, and never will—The cry of "I'm afraid" has always been heard—Opposition to new ideas—How Fear may be defeated—Fear a humbug and a bugaboo, without any real power over us except that which we allow him.

Many of you have read Edward Bulwer Lytton's occult story, "Zanoni," and remember the "Dweller of the Threshold," that frightful monster which confronted the neophyte, Glyndon, in the secret chamber of the master, Mejnour, and of which Mejnour speaks when he says: "Amidst the dwellers of the Threshold is One, too, surpassing in malignity and hatred all her tribe—one whose eyes have paralyzed the bravest and whose power increases over the spirit precisely in proportion to its fear."

In another chapter Glyndon seeks to penetrate the mysteries of the secret chamber and meets the hideous keeper of the door, which' is described thus: "* * * The casement became darkened with some object undistinguishable at the first gaze, but which sufficed mysteriously to change into ineffable horror the delight he had before experienced. By degrees this object shaped itself to his sight. It was that of a human head, covered with a dark veil, through which glared with livid and demoniac fire eyes that froze the marrow of his bones. Nothing else of the face was distinguishable—nothing but those intolerable eyes. * * * It seemed rather to crawl as some vast misshapen reptile; and, pausing at length, it cowered beside the table which held the mystic volume and again fixed its eyes through the filmy veil on the rash invoker. * * * Clinging with the grasp of agony to the wall, his hair erect, his eye-balls starting, he still gazed back upon that appalling gaze. The Image spoke to him—his soul rather than his ear comprehended the words it said: 'Thou hast entered the immeasurable region. I am the Dweller of the Threshold'."

Those familiar with occult symbols and figures recognize in Lytton's Dweller of the Threshold that enemy of Man's progress—that frightful figure that stands before the door to freedom—FEAR.

Fear is the first and great enemy to be overcome by the man or woman who wishes to escape from bondage and attain Freedom. The door to Freedom is pointed out and the seeker makes a few steps in that direction, but is halted by the sight of the malignant Dweller of the Threshold—FEAR. Lytton has not painted it in too frightful form—words cannot describe the hideousness of this monster.

Fear stands in the road of all progress—all advancement—escape. Fear is at the bottom of all of Man's failures—sorrows—unhappinesses. The Fear of the race keeps it in bondage—the Fear of the individual keeps him a slave. Until Fear is overcome there can be no advancement for either individual or race. This enemy must be overcome before there can be escape. And it *can* be overcome by those who will face it calmly and boldly. Look Fear square in the eyes and her eyes drop and she retreats before you. Assert the I AM, and know, in the depths of your soul, that nothing can injure the real "I," and Fear flies before you, fearing that you will conquer her and bind her with chains—she knows the power of the I AM consciousness.

When a man allows Fear to enter his heart he attracts to him all that which he fears. Fear is a powerful magnet and exercises a wonderful attracting power. Besides this it paralyzes the efforts and energy of the man and prevents him from doing that which he could easily do were he free of the monster. Man succeeds in proportion as he frees himself from Fear. Show me the successful man and I will show you a man who has *dared* and who has turned his back upon Fear.

Take your own life, for instance. You have had many opportunities offered you which you have allowed to pass you because of Fear. You have met with a fair degree of success, and, at the last moment, when the prize was in sight, you have drawn back your hand and fled to the rear. Why? Because you "lost your nerve" and Fear entered your heart. When the microbe of Fear enters the system the entire body is paralyzed.

Fear is the parent of the entire brood of negative thoughts which keep men in bondage. From her womb spring Worry, Jealousy, Hate, Malice, Envy, Uncharitableness, Bigotry, Intolerance, Condemnation, Anger and the rest of the foul brood. You doubt this, do you? Well, let us see. You do not worry about things unless you fear them; you do not feel jealous unless fear is also present; hate is always mingled with fear and springs from it—one does not hate a thing that is beyond the power of hurting him; envy shows its origin; bigotry, intolerance and condemnation all arise from fear—persecution begins only when the object is feared; a close analysis will show that anger springs from a vague sense of fear of the thing which causes the anger— a thing that is not feared causes amusement and derision rather than anger. Analyze closely and you will find that all of these negative, hurtful thoughts bear a close family resemblance to their parent—Fear. And if you will start in to work and will abolish Fear the foul brood of youngsters will die for want of nourishment.

Fear has hypnotized the race for ages, and its effects are as noticeable now as ever. We have taken in Fear with our mother's milk—yes, even before birth we have been cursed with this thing. We have had it suggested into us from childhood. The "ifs," "supposings," "buts," "what-ifs" and "aren't-you-afraids" have always been with us. We have been taught to fear everything in the heavens above, the earth beneath and the waters under the earth. The bugaboos of childhood—the things-to-be-feared of manhood—are all off the same piece. We are told all our lives that "the goblins will catch you if you don't look out." Turn which way we may the suggestions of Fear are constantly being poured into us. Any one who knows the power of repeated suggestions can realize what all this has meant to the world. The brave band of New Thought people—Don't Worry people—and others of this line of thought, are doing much toward pouring a stream of clear, living water into the muddy, stagnant pool of Fearthought that the world has allowed to accumulate, and others are adding to the stream every day, but the pool is enormous.

Fear never accomplished any good and never will. It is a negative thought which has dragged its slimy form along the ages, seeking to devour all which promised good to Mankind. It is the greatest enemy of progress—the sworn foe of Freedom. The cry, "I'm afraid," has always been heard, and it is only when some man or woman, or a number of them, has dared to laugh in its face, that some bold deed has been done that has caused the world to go forward a notch or so. Let some one advance a new idea calculated to benefit the world, and at once you hear the cry of Fear, with the accompanying yells of the whelps, Hate and Anger, filling the air and awakening echoing yells, growls and snarls from all the Fear-kennels within hearing distance. Let any one try to do a thing in a new way—improve upon some accepted plan—teach the Truth in a new way—and the yell goes up. Fear is the curse of the race.

The man who is in bondage to Fear is a very slave, and no crueler master ever existed. In proportion to his fear, Man

sinks in the mud. And the pathetic, although somewhat humor-
ous, part of it all is, that all the time the man has sufficient power
to rise up and smite his task-master a blow between the eyes
which will cause him to retreat in a hurry. Man is like a young
elephant which has not yet recognized its strength. When one
once realizes that nothing can hurt him, Fear flees from him.
The man who recognizes just what he is, and what is his place
in the Universe, parts company with Fear forever. And, before
he reaches this stage, Fear loses its hold upon him as he ad-
vances step by step toward that recognition.

And not only on this plane may Fear be defeated, but even
on the lower plane of self-interest and self-advancement Fear may
be gotten rid of. When Man recognizes that Fear is a sort of
home-made, pumpkin-headed jack-o'-lantern, instead of the fiery-
eyed monster of the night he had supposed it to be, he will walk
up to it and knock it off the fence post where it had been placed
to frighten him. He will see that the things that happen are never
so bad as the things that were feared. He will see that the Fear
of a thing is worse than the thing itself. He will see that, as the
anticipation of a desired thing is greater than the realization, so
is the anticipation of a feared thing worse than the happening
of it. And he will find that the majority of feared things do not
happen. And he will find that even when things do happen, some-
how matters are straightened out so that we bear the burden
much better than we had dreamt would be possible—God not
only tempers the wind to the shorn lamb, but he tempers the shorn
lamb to the wind.

And Man finds that the very fearing of a thing often brings
it upon him while a fearless mental attitude sends the thing flying
away often at the last moment. Job cried out, "The thing that
I feared hath come upon me."

Some one has said, and I have often repeated it: "There is nothing to be feared but Fear." Well, I go further than that now
and say that there is no sense in fearing even Fear, for, as terri-
ble as he appears on the outside, he is made of the flimsiest ma-
terial on the inside. He is "a lath painted to resemble iron."
A few strong blows will smash him. He is a fraud—a yellow
dog wearing a lion's skin. Stand up before him and smile
boldly in his face—look him in the eyes and smile. Do not mind
his frightful form—his hideous mask—he is a weakling when
matched with Courage and Confidence. All these negative
thoughts are weaklings when compared with their opposites on
the positive plane.

Would you know how to get rid of Fear? Then listen. The
way to get rid of Fear is to ignore his existence and to carry before you, and with you always, the ideals of Courage and Confi-

dence. Confidence in the great plan of which you are a part. Courage in your strength as a part of the whole. Confidence in the workings of the Law. Courage in your ability to work in accordance with the Law. Confidence in your destiny. Courage in your knowledge of the reality of the Whole and the illusions of separateness. Courage and Confidence arising from the knowledge of the Law of Attraction and the power of Thought-force. ·Courage and Confidence in your knowledge that the Positive always overcomes the Negative.

Men often say·-that The New Thought principles are beyond them—that they cannot comprehend—that they want something that will be of use to them ·in their every day lives. Well, here is something for such people. This idea of the abolishing of Fear will make them over and will give them a peace of mind that they have never been conscious of before. It will give them sweet sleep after business hours; it will give them an even mind during business hours; it will make their paths smoother and will obviate friction: it will soon be used to cause things to "come their way." And while it is doing these things for them it will be making better men of them. It will be preparing them for the recognition of higher truths.

You neophyte, who are standing at the door of the secret chamber. longing to pass through its portals and thence to knowledge and freedom and power, be not dismayed at the sight of the Dweller of the Threshold. He is merely "gotten up for the occasion." Smile in his face and gaze steadily into his eyes and you will see what an old humbug he is. Push him aside and enter into the room of knowledge. Beyond that are other rooms for you, which you will pass through in turn. Leave the Dweller for timid mortals who are afraid that the "goblins will get them." Faint heart never won fair lady nor anything else worth having in this world. And "none but the brave deserve the fair," or anything else. So drop your whining cry of "I Can't" or your sniveling "I'm afraid," and, shouting boldly, "I CAN AND I WILL," brush past the Dweller of the Threshold, crowd him up against the door-post with your shoulder and walk into the Room.

CPSIA information can be obtained
at www.ICGtesting.com
Printed in the USA
LVRC011333070420
652505LV00024B/538